Aikido Terminology

An essential reference guide in both English and Japanese

Michael W Taylor

© 2004 by Michael W Taylor. All rights reserved.

All rights reserved. No part of this publication can be reproduced, stored in a retrieval system, or transmitted in any form or by any means, electronic, mechanical, photocopying, recording or otherwise, without the prior permission of the publishers and/or authors.

While every precaution has been taken in the preparation of this book, the publisher assumes no responsibilities for errors or omissions, or for damages resulting from the use of information contained herein.

Join the author's Aikido club online!
http://sports.groups.yahoo.com/group/aikido2/

Contents

Introduction	4
Special Thanks	4
How To Use This Book	5
Explanation of the Kanji Pages	6
Chapter 1 The terms "Aikido" & "Aikido Practitioner"	7
Chapter 2 Stances	11
Chapter 3 Grasps	17
Chapter 4 Basic Strikes	25
Chapter 5 Basic Falls and Rolls	31
Chapter 6 Fundamental Techniques	33
Chapter 7 Aikido Actions	41
Chapter 8 Part of the Body	51
Chapter 9 Weapons/Aiki-Wear/Ranks/Special Training	55
Chapter 10 People	61
Chapter 11 Places	67
Chapter 12 Miscellaneous	71
Index	82
Credits	90

Introduction

This book has been created for *all* practitioners of Aikido. Included is a description of all fundamental Aikido terms, the Japanese kanji characters as used in Aikido, their meaning and cross-reference to a kanji guidebook for those who wish to study their meaning further.

An attempt has been made to present information in a logical sequence. Also, where a term is comprised of more than one kanji character, each character is defined individually.

It is my hope that you find this body of work useful and interesting as you pursue the art of Aikido. Understanding the meaning of what you are saying (or what your teacher is saying) will increase your enjoyment of training and further open your mind to *understanding*.

Special Thanks

Many thanks to everyone I have had the pleasure of coming into contact with in martial arts and had the privilege to learn from. But I must say a special thanks to David Monroe, (www.sof-stx.com), Carmen Pelusi (Eight Winds Aikido Society – Gautier, Mississippi) and Yasuo Hashimoto – my first teacher in Japan. Also, special thanks to my friend Mr. Katsumi Sakai for taking time on a very hot day to climb the steps up to Wakayama castle to take the photos for this book. And thank you to my beautiful wife Miyako for climbing up and taking the pictures. The list of everyone else is long and I am grateful to them as well. As I have received - so must I give.

How To Use This Book

The book is broken down into the following logical categories: stances, grasps, strikes, falls and rolls, fundamental techniques, various Aikido actions, body parts, weapons, Aiki-wear, ranks, special training times, and finally, miscellaneous items that do not fit into any of the above categories.

Most importantly, all terms are listed in alphabetical order in the index at the end of the book - first by the Romaji (English) spelling of the Japanese term, and second, by the English word for the Japanese term. Therefore; all terms can be quickly and conveniently referenced. So next time you are in your Aikido class and you hear something you don't understand, simply flip to the index and look up the word in the Romaji index and voila!

Chapters 2 through 6 are presented in the order in which one would be taught if starting at a dojo in Japan - developing a solid foundation of the basics before moving on to each successive level. In other words, you must learn the grasps and how to perform them properly, then the stances and how to stand properly, and so on and so forth. Certainly the art has evolved over time, however, the fundamentals remain largely unchanged and provide the cornerstone on which to build all Aikido techniques. Therefore, I encourage you to have patience and be thankful for the teacher who has you work the "basic" techniques over and over. Remember, in Japanese calligraphy, the most difficult character, and perhaps most profound, to write is the number "one", a single horizontal stroke.

Explanation of the Kanji Pages

1.
2.
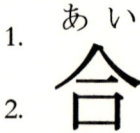

3. Meaning: to fit, put together

4. Romaji: **ai**

5. Phonetic: ah ee

6. Guide: 159

1. The presented kanji character represented in hiragana as a phonetic guide.

2. The kanji character.

3. The English meaning.

4. The romanization of the sound. In other words, how the word is written in English. **NOTE:** There are, in many cases, more pronunciations for each kanji presented here. No attempt is made to present all of them in this book. For further study I highly recommend, **Kanji & Kana, A Handbook of the Japanese Writing System**, ISBN 0-8048-2077-5 by Wolfgang Hadamitzky and Mark Spahn. Tuttle Publishing. www.tuttlepublishing.com

5. The phonetic presentation of the word or sound.

6. The number of the character as listed in **Kanji & Kana, A Handbook of the Japanese Writing System**, ISBN 0-8048-2077-5 by Wolfgang Hadamitzky and Mark Spahn. Tuttle Publishing. www.tuttlepublishing.com Looking the character up in this book will give you all of the readings, meanings, stroke order and several compound examples.

Chapter 1

The terms "Aikido" & "Aikido Practitioner"

1. Aikido 合氣道 The Japanese martial art of Aikido p. 8
2. Aikidoka 合氣道家 A practitioner of Aikido p. 9

1. 合氣道
あ い き ど う

Meaning: The art developed by Morihei Ueshiba
Romaji: **aikido-**
Phonetic: ah ee kee doe oo
Guide: 159, 134, 149

1a. 合
あ い

Meaning: to fit, put together
Romaji: **ai**
Phonetic: ah ee
Guide: 159

1b. 氣
き

Meaning: spirit, soul, mood
Romaji: **ki**
Phonetic: kee
Guide: 134

1c. 道
ど う

Meaning: way, path
Romaji: **do-**
Phonetic: doe oo
Guide: 149

2. 合氣道家
あ い き ど う か

Meaning: one who participates in Aikido
Romaji: **aikido-ka**
Phonetic: ah ee kee doe oo kah
Guide: 159, 134, 149, 165

2a. 家
いえ

Meaning: house, family
Romaji: **ie**
Phonetic: ee eh
Guide: 165

Me and the grandson of O-sensei, Moriteru Ueshiba, in Tanabe, Japan. I met him several times over the course of seven years. He is a very kind man.

Later I had the pleasure of meeting the son of O-sensei, Kishomaru Ueshiba, in Wakayama city, Japan. Also pictured is the man who taught me the most about Aikido – Sensei Yasuo Hashimoto of the Musota dojo. Thank you sensei for everything!

Chapter 2

Stances

<ruby>半身<rt>はんみ</rt></ruby>

1. Half-Facing Stance 半身 Hanmi p. 12
2. Right Half-Facing Stance 右半身 Migi hanmi p. 13
3. Left Half-Facing Stance 左半身 Hidari hanmi p. 14
4. Same Foot Forward Stance 相半身 Ai hanmi p. 15
5. Opposite Foot Forward Stance 逆半身 Gyaku hanmi p. 16

はんみ
1. 半身

Meaning: half-facing stance
Romaji: **hanmi**
Phonetic: ha n mee
Guide: 88, 59

はん 1a. 半	み 1b. 身
Meaning: half Romaji: **han** Phonetic: ha n Guide: 88	Meaning: body Romaji: **mi** Phonetic: mee Guide: 59

12

2. 右半身
<small>みぎ はん み</small>

Meaning: right foot forward half-facing stance
Romaji: **migi hanmi**
Phonetic: mih gee ha n mee
Guide: 76,88, 59

2a. 右
<small>みぎ</small>

Meaning: right
Romaji: **migi**
Phonetic: mih gee
Guide: 76

2b. 半
<small>はん</small>

Meaning: half
Romaji: **han**
Phonetic: ha n
Guide: 88

2c. 身
<small>み</small>

Meaning: body
Romaji: **mi**
Phonetic: mee
Guide: 59

3. 左半身
ひだり は ん み

Meaning: left foot forward half-facing stance
Romaji: **hidari hanmi**
Phonetic: hee dah ree ha n mee
Guide: 75, 88, 59

3a. 左
ひだり

Meaning: left
Romaji: **hidari**
Phonetic: hee dah ree
Guide: 75

3b. 半
はん

Meaning: half
Romaji: **han**
Phonetic: ha n
Guide: 88

3c. 身
み

Meaning: body
Romaji: **mi**
Phonetic: mee
Guide: 59

4. 相半身
あい はん み

Meaning: partners have same foot forward half-facing stance
Romaji: **ai hanmi**
Phonetic: ah ee ha n mee
Guide: 146, 88, 59

4a. 相
あい

Meaning: together
Romaji: **ai**
Phonetic: ah ee
Guide: 146

4b. 半
はん

Meaning: half
Romaji: **han**
Phonetic: ha n
Guide: 88

4c. 身
み

Meaning: body
Romaji: **mi**
Phonetic: mee
Guide: 59

5. 逆半身
_{ぎゃく はん み}

Meaning: partners have opposite foot forward half-facing stance
Romaji: **gyaku hanmi**
Phonetic: gee ya koo ha n mee
Guide: 444, 88, 59

5a. 逆
_{ぎゃく}

Meaning: opposite
Romaji: **gyaku**
Phonetic: gee ya koo
Guide: 444

5b. 半
_{はん}

Meaning: half
Romaji: **han**
Phonetic: ha n
Guide: 88

5c. 身
_み

Meaning: body
Romaji: **mi**
Phonetic: mee
Guide: 59

Chapter 3

Grasps

持ち方

1. Grasping Method 持ち方 Mochi kata p. 18
2. Non-Crossed One-Handed Grasp 片手持ち Katate mochi p. 19
3. Two on Two, Two-Handed Grasp 両手持ち Ryote mochi p. 20
4. Crossed One-Handed Grasp 交差持ち Ko-sa mochi p. 21
5. Two-On-One, Hand Grasp 諸手持ち Morote mochi p. 22
6. Collar Grasp 襟持ち Eri mochi p. 23
7. Two-On-Two, Hand Grasp From Behind 後取り Ushiro dori p. 24

1. 持ち方
も　かた

Meaning: grasping method
Romaji: **mo(chi) kata**
Phonetic: moe (chee) kah tah
Guide: 451, 70

1a. 持つ
も

Meaning: to have, possess, hold
Romaji: **mo(tsu)**
Phonetic: moe (tsoo)
Guide: 451

1b. 方
かた

Meaning: direction; person; method
Romaji: **kata**
Phonetic: kah tah
Guide: 70

2. 片手持ち
かたてもち

Meaning: one-handed grasp with left on right or right on left
Romaji: **kata te mo(chi)**
Phonetic: kah tah teh moe (chee)
Guide: 1045, 57, 451

2a. 片
かた

Meaning: one of two
Romaji: **kata**
Phonetic: kah tah
Guide: 1045

2b. 手
て

Meaning: hand
Romaji: **te**
Phonetic: teh
Guide: 57

2c. 持つ
も

Meaning: have, hold
Romaji: **mo(tsu)**
Phonetic: moe (tsoo)
Guide: 451

19

3. 両手持ち
りょう て も

Meaning: two-handed grasp with two on two
Romaji: **ryo-te mo(chi)**
Phonetic: ree yoe oo teh moe (chee)
Guide: 200, 57, 451

3a. 両
りょう

Meaning: both
Romaji: **ryo-**
Phonetic: ree yoe oo
Guide: 200

3b. 手
て

Meaning: hand
Romaji: **te**
Phonetic: teh
Guide: 57

3c. 持つ
も

Meaning: to have, hold
Romaji: **mo(tsu)**
Phonetic: moe (tsoo)
Guide: 451

4. 交差持ち
こう さ も

Meaning: cross-handed grasp with one on one
Romaji: **ko-sa mo(chi)**
Phonetic: koe oo sah moe (chee)
Guide: 114, 658, 451

4a. 交 (こう)

Meaning: intersection
Romaji: **ko-**
Phonetic: koe oo
Guide: 114

4b. 差 (さ)

Meaning: difference
Romaji: **sa**
Phonetic: sah
Guide: 658

4c. 持つ (も)

Meaning: to have, hold
Romaji: **mo(tsu)**
Phonetic: moe (tsoo)
Guide: 451

21

5. 諸手持ち
もろ　て　　も

Meaning: two-handed grasp with two on one
Romaji: **morote mo(chi)**
Phonetic: moe roe teh moe (chee)
Guide: 861, 57, 451

5a. 諸
もろ

Meaning: all, various
Romaji: **moro**
Phonetic: moe roe
Guide: 861

5b. 手
て

Meaning: hand
Romaji: **te**
Phonetic: teh
Guide: 57

5c. 持つ
も

Meaning: to have, hold
Romaji: **mo(tsu)**
Phonetic: moe (tsoo)
Guide: 451

6. 襟持ち
<small>えり も</small>

Meaning: collar grasp
Romaji: **eri mo(chi)**
Phonetic: eh ree moe (chee)
Guide: 1537, 451

6a. 襟
<small>えり</small>

Meaning: collar, lapel
Romaji: **eri**
Phonetic: eh ree
Guide: 1537

6b. 持つ
<small>も</small>

Meaning: to have, possess, hold
Romaji: **mo(tsu)**
Phonetic: moe (tsoo)
Guide: 451

23

7. 後取り
うしろ ど

Meaning: grasping both hands from behind
Romaji: **ushiro do(ri)**
Phonetic: oo shee roe doe (ree)
Guide: 48, 65

7a. 後
うしろ

Meaning: behind
Romaji: **ushiro**
Phonetic: oo shee roe
Guide: 48

7b. 取る
と

Meaning: to take
Romaji: **to(ru)**
Phonetic: toe (roo)
Guide: 65

Chapter 4

Basic Strikes

基本の打ち方

1. Striking Method 打ち方 Uchikata p. 26
2. Front Strike 正面打ち Shomenuchi p. 27
3. Diagonal Strike 横面打ち Yokomenuchi p. 28
4. Punch 突き Tsuki p. 29
5. Face Punch 顔面突き Ganmenzuki p. 29
6. Kick 蹴り Keri p. 29
7. Strikes 当身 Atemi p. 29

1. 打ち方
<small>う　か た</small>

Meaning: striking method
Romaji: **u(chi) kata**
Phonetic: oo (chee) kah tah
Guide: 1020, 70

1a. 打つ
<small>う</small>

Meaning: to strike, hit
Romaji: **u(tsu)**
Phonetic: oo (tsoo)
Guide: 1020

1b. 方
<small>か た</small>

Meaning: direction; person; method
Romaji: **kata**
Phonetic: kah tah
Guide: 70

2. 正面打ち
しょうめん う

Meaning: centered vertical downward strike from the front
Romaji: sho-men u(chi)
Phonetic: shoe oo me n oo (chee)
Guide: 275, 274, 1020

2a. 正
しょう

Meaning: correct
Romaji: **sho-**
Phonetic: shoe oo
Guide: 275

2b. 面
めん

Meaning: face, mask
Romaji: **men**
Phonetic: me n
Guide: 274

2c. 正面
しょうめん

Meaning: the front, front side
Romaji: **sho-men**
Phonetic: shoe oo me n
Guide: 275, 274

2d. 打つ
う

Meaning: to strike, hit
Romaji: **u(tsu)**
Phonetic: oo (tsoo)
Guide: 1020

27

3. 横面打ち
よこめん う

Meaning: vertical downward strike cutting down at a diagonal
Romaji: **yokomen u(chi)**
Phonetic: yoe koe meh n oo (chee)
Guide: 781, 274, 1020

3a. 横
よこ

Meaning: side
Romaji: **yoko**
Phonetic: yoe koe
Guide: 781

3b. 横面
よこめん

Meaning: the side
Romaji: **yokomen**
Phonetic: yoe koe meh n
Guide: 781, 274

3c. 打つ
う

Meaning: to strike, hit
Romaji: **u(tsu)**
Phonetic: oo (tsoo)
Guide: 1020

4. 突<ruby>き<rt>つ</rt></ruby>

Meaning: punch
Romaji: **tsu(ki)**
Phonetic: tsoo (kee)
Guide: 898

4a. 突<ruby>く<rt>つ</rt></ruby>

Meaning: to thrust, poke, strike
Romaji: **tsu(ku)**
Phonetic: tsoo (koo)
Guide: 898

5. <ruby>顔面<rt>がんめん</rt></ruby>突<ruby>き<rt>づ</rt></ruby>

Meaning: face punch
Romaji: **ganmen zu(ki)**
Phonetic: gah n meh n zoo (kee)
Guide: 277, 274, 898

5a. <ruby>顔面<rt>がんめん</rt></ruby>

Meaning: face
Romaji: **ganmen**
Phonetic: gah n meh n
Guide: 277, 274

5b. <ruby>顔<rt>かお</rt></ruby>

Meaning: face
Romaji: **kao**
Phonetic: kah oe
Guide: 277

5c. <ruby>面<rt>めん</rt></ruby>

Meaning: side
Romaji: **men**
Phonetic: meh n
Guide: 274

6. <ruby>蹴<rt>け</rt></ruby>り

Meaning: a kick
Romaji: **ke(ri)**
Phonetic: keh (ree)
Guide: * 7d12.2

6a. <ruby>蹴<rt>け</rt></ruby>る

Meaning: to kick
Romaji: **ke(ru)**
Phonetic: keh (roo)
Guide: * 7d12.2

7. <ruby>当<rt>あ</rt></ruby>て<ruby>身<rt>み</rt></ruby>

Meaning: strikes to the body
Romaji: **a(te)mi**
Phonetic: ah (teh) mee
Guide: 77, 59 (see page 12)

7a. <ruby>当<rt>あ</rt></ruby>たる

Meaning: to hit, be on target
Romaji: **a(taru)**
Phonetic: ah (tah) roo
Guide: 77

Wakayama castle as seen from the top of the hill in Okakoen (Oka Park). Walk down the hill and you are at the Okakoen Aikido Dojo! See you there bright and early at 6:30am!

Chapter 5

Basic Falls and Rolls

<ruby>基本<rt>きほん</rt>受<rt>う</rt>け身<rt>み</rt></ruby>
基本受け身

1. Defensive fall 受け身 Ukemi p. 32
2. Forward roll 前受け身 Maeukemi p. 32
3. Backward roll 後ろ受け身 Ushiroukemi p. 32

1. 受け身

う　み

Meaning: a defensive fall
Romaji: **u(ke)mi**
Phonetic: oo (keh) mee
Guide: 260, 59 (see page 12)

1a. 受ける

う

Meaning: to receive, accept
Romaji: **u(keru)**
Phonetic: oo (keh) roo
Guide: 260

2. 前受け身

まえ う　み

Meaning: forward roll
Romaji: **mae u(ke)mi**
Phonetic: mie oo (keh) mee
Guide: 47, 260, 59 (see page 12)

2a. 前

まえ

Meaning: front
Romaji: **mae**
Phonetic: mah eh
Guide: 47

3. 後受け身

うしろ う　み

Meaning: backward roll
Romaji: **ushiro u(ke)mi**
Phonetic: oo shee roe oo (keh) mee
Guide: 48, 59 (see page 12)

3a. 後

うしろ

Meaning: rear
Romaji: **ushiro**
Phonetic: oo shee roe
Guide: 48

Chapter 6

Fundamental Techniques 基本技

A. Fundamental Techniques

1. Fixed position technique 固め技 Katame waza p. 34
2. Flowing technique 流れ技 Nagare waza p. 34
3. Sitting technique 座り技 Suwari waza p. 34
4. Standing technique 立ち技 Tachi waza p. 34
5. One sitting/one standing tech. 半身半立技 Hanmihandachi waza p. 35

B. Fundamental Controls

1. The first control 一教 Ikkyo- p. 35,36
2. The second control 二教 Nikkyo- p. 35,36
3. The third control 三教 Sankkyo- p. 35,36
4. The fourth control 四教 Yonkkyo- p. 35,36

C. Fundamental Throws

1. Wrist twist throw 小手返し Kotegaeshi p. 37
2. Four directions throw 四方投げ Shiho-nage p. 37
3. Heaven & Earth throw 天地投げ Tenchi nage p. 38
4. Entering techniques 入り身投げ Irimi nage p. 38
5. Breathe throw 呼吸投げ Kokyu- nage p. 39
6. Hip throw 腰投げ Koshi nage p. 39

A. Fundamental Techniques

1. 固め技
かた・わざ

Meaning: technique ending in a fixed position
Romaji: **kata(me) waza**
Phonetic: kah tah (meh) wah zah
Guide: 972, 871 (see page 78)

1a. 固める
かた

Meaning: to make solid, harden
Romaji: **kata(meru)**
Phonetic: kah tah (meh roo)
Guide: 972

2. 流れ技
なが・わざ

Meaning: a technique that flows
Romaji: **naga(re) waza**
Phonetic: nah gah (reh) wah zah
Guide: 247, 871 (see page 78)

2a. 流れる
なが

Meaning: to flow
Romaji: **naga(reru)**
Phonetic: nah gah (reh roo)
Guide: 247

3. 座り技
すわ・わざ

Meaning: sitting technique
Romaji: **suwa(ri) waza**
Phonetic: soo wah (ree) wah zah
Guide: 786, 871 (see page 78)

3a. 座る
すわ

Meaning: to sit down
Romaji: **suwa(ru)**
Phonetic: soo wah (roo)
Guide: 786

4. 立ち技
た・わざ

Meaning: standing technique
Romaji: **ta(chi) waza**
Phonetic: tah (chee) wah zah
Guide: 121, 871 (see page 78)

4a. 立つ
た

Meaning: to stand
Romaji: **ta(tsu)**
Phonetic: tah (tsoo)
Guide: 121

5. 半身半立ち技
<ruby>はんみはんだち わざ</ruby>

Meaning: techniques done with one sitting and one standing
Romaji: **hanmi han da(chi) waza**
Phonetic: hah n mee hah n dah (chee) wah zah
Guide: 88, 59, 88, 121, 871 (see page 78)

B. Fundamental Controls

1. 一教押さえ
いっきょう お

Meaning: First Control
Romaji: **ikkyo- o(sae)**
Phonetic: ee kkyoe oe (sah eh)
Guide: 2, 245, 986

2. 二教押さえ
に きょう お

Meaning: Second Control
Romaji: **nikyo- o(sae)**
Phonetic: nee kyoe oe (sah eh)
Guide: 3, 245, 986

3. 三教押さえ
さんきょう お

Meaning: Third Control
Romaji: **sankyo- o(sae)**
Phonetic: sah n kyoe oe (sah eh)
Guide: 4, 245, 986

4. 四教押さえ
よんきょう お

Meaning: Fourth Control
Romaji: **yonkyo- o(sae)**
Phonetic: yoh n kyoe oe (sah eh)
Guide: 6, 245, 986

1a. 一
いち

Meaning: one
Romaji: **ichi**
Phonetic: ee chee
Guide: 2

2a. 二
に

Meaning: two
Romaji: **ni**
Phonetic: nee
Guide: 3

3a. 三
さん

Meaning: three
Romaji: **san**
Phonetic: sah n
Guide: 4

4a. 四
よん

Meaning: four
Romaji: **yon**
Phonetic: yoe n
Guide: 6

5a. 教える
おし

Meaning: to teach
Romaji: **oshi(eru)**
Phonetic: oe shee eh roo
Guide: 245

6a. 押さえる
お

Meaning: to restrain
Romaji: **o(saeru)**
Phonetic: oe (sah eh roo)
Guide: 986

C. Fundamental Throws

1. 小手返し
<ruby>こ</ruby> <ruby>て</ruby> <ruby>がえ</ruby>

Meaning: wrist twist throw
Romaji: **kotegae(shi)**
Phonetic: koe teh gah eh shee
Guide: 27, 274, 442

1a. 小
こう

Meaning: small
Romaji: **ko-**
Phonetic: koe oo
Guide: 27

1b. 手
て

Meaning: hand
Romaji: **te**
Phonetic: teh
Guide: 274

1c. 返す
かえ

Meaning: to return
Romaji: **kae(su)**
Phonetic: kah eh (soo)
Guide: 442

2. 四方投げ
し ほう な

Meaning: four-direction throw
Romaji: **shiho-na(ge)**
Phonetic: shee hoe oo nah (geh)
Guide: 6, 70, 1021

2a. 四方
し ほう

Meaning: four directions
Romaji: **shiho-**
Phonetic: shee hoe oo
Guide: 6, 70

2b. 投げる
な

Meaning: to throw
Romaji: **na(geru)**
Phonetic: nah (geh roo)
Guide: 1021

3. 天地投げ
てんちな

Meaning: heaven and earth throw – one hand up and one down
Romaji: **tenchi na(ge)**
Phonetic: teh n chee nah (geh)
Guide: 141, 118, 1021

3a. 天
てん

Meaning: heaven
Romaji: **ten**
Phonetic: teh n
Guide: 141

3b. 地
ち

Meaning: earth
Romaji: **chi**
Phonetic: chee
Guide: 118

3c. 投げる
な

Meaning: to throw
Romaji: **na(geru)**
Phonetic: nah (geh roo)
Guide: 1021

4. 入り身投げ
いみな

Meaning: to move the body in and throw
Romaji: **i(ri)mi na(ge)**
Phonetic: ee (ree) mee nah (geh)
Guide: 52, 59(see page 12), 1021

4a. 入る
はい

Meaning: to enter
Romaji: **hai(ru)**
Phonetic: ha ee (roo)
Guide: 52

4b. 投げる
な

Meaning: to throw
Romaji: **na(geru)**
Phonetic: nah (geh roo)
Guide: 1021

5. 呼吸投げ
<small>こ きゅう な</small>

Meaning: breathe control throw
Romaji: **kokyu- na(ge)**
Phonetic: koe kee yoo nah (geh)
Guide: 1254, 1256, 1021

5a. 呼吸
<small>こ きゅう</small>

Meaning: breathe
Romaji: **kokyu-**
Phonetic: koe kee yoo
Guide: 1254, 1256

5b. 投げる
<small>な</small>

Meaning: to throw
Romaji: **na(geru)**
Phonetic: nah (geh roo)
Guide: 1021

6. 腰投げ
<small>こし な</small>

Meaning: hip throw
Romaji: **koshi na(ge)**
Phonetic: koe shee nah (geh)
Guide: 1298, 1021

6a. 腰
<small>こし</small>

Meaning: hips
Romaji: **koshi**
Phonetic: koe shee
Guide: 1298

6b. 投げる
<small>な</small>

Meaning: to throw
Romaji: **na(geru)**
Phonetic: nah (geh roo)
Guide: 1021

Don't I look lovely? You can tell I just finished working out because my hakama is falling off! This poster has been hanging in Okakoen Dojo since 1988. This picture was taken in July of 2004.

Chapter 7
Aiki-Actions 合気道の行動

A. Warm-Up Actions 準備運動 Junbi undo-

    1. Rowing the boat 漕ぎ船運動 Kogibuneundo- p. 42

    2. Spirit shake 振り霊 Furitama p. 43

B. Etiquette Actions 礼式行動 Reishiki no ko-do-

    1. Sitting 正座 Seiza p. 44

    2. Bowing 礼 Rei p. 44

    3. Requesting お願いします Onegaishimasu p. 44

    4. Thanking 有り難うございました Arigato-gozaimashita p. 44,45

C. Misc. Actions その他の行動 Sono ta no ko-do-

    1. Practice 稽古 Keiko p. 45

    2. Spirit shout 氣合 Kiai p. 45

    3. Fundamental movement 基本動作 Kihondo-sa p. 46

    4. Posture 構え Kamae p. 47

    5. Purification 禊 Misogi p. 47

    6. Meditation 黙想 Mokuso- p. 47

    7. Front 表 Omote p. 48

    8. Rear 裏 Ura p. 48

    9. Round robin 乱取り Randori p. 48

    10. Practice 練習 Renshu- p. 48

    11. Four directions cut 四方切り Shiho-giri p. 49

    12. Knee walk 膝行 Shikko- p. 49

    13. Feet slide 摺足 Suriashi p. 49,50

    14. Body movements 体裁き Taisabaki p. 50

    15. Turn 転換 Tenkan p. 50

A. Warm-Up Actions

こ　ぶねうんどう
1. 漕ぎ船運動

Meaning: a grounding warm-up exercise that resembles rowing a boat
Romaji: **ko(gi) bune undo-**
Phonetic: koe (gee) boo nae oo n doe oo
Guide: * 3a11.7, 376, 439, 231

こ 1a. 漕ぐ	ふね 1b. 船
Meaning: to row a boat	Meaning: a boat, ship
Romaji: **ko(gu)**	Romaji: **fune**
Phonetic: koe (goo)	Phonetic: foo nae
Guide: * 3a11.7	Guide: 376

2. 振り霊
ふ　たま

Meaning: a grounding warm-up exercise to "shake down your spirit"
Romaji: **fu(ri) tama**
Phonetic: foo (ree) tah mah
Guide: 954, 1168

2a. 振る
ふ

Meaning: to wave, shake
Romaji: **fu(ru)**
Phonetic: foo (roo)
Guide: 954

2b. 霊
たま

Meaning: soul, spirit
Romaji: **tama**
Phonetic: tah mah
Guide: 1168

B. Etiquette Actions

1. 正座 <small>せいざ</small>

Meaning: to sit with legs tucked under and big toes just touching
Romaji: **seiza**
Phonetic: seh ee zah
Guide: 275 (see page 27), 786 (see page 34)

2. 礼 <small>れい</small>

Meaning: to bow in courteous salutation
Romaji: **rei**
Phonetic: rae ee
Guide: 620

3. お願いします <small>ねが</small>

Meaning: a "please" expression one says when bowing to sensei at the beginning of class and when bowing to each partner before beginning to train
Romaji: **(o)nega(ishimasu)**
Phonetic: (oe) neh gah (ee shee mah soo)
Guide: 581

3a. 願う <small>ねが</small>

Meaning: to petition, request, desire
Romaji: **nega(u)**
Phonetic: neh gah (oo)
Guide: 581

4. 有り難うございました <small>あ がと</small>

Meaning: "thank you" said at the end of class to sensei and when bowing to each partner after training with them
Romaji: **a(ri)gato(-gozaimashita)**
Phonetic: ah (ree) gah toe oo (goe zah ee mah shee tah)
Guide: 265,557

4a. 有る
あ

Meaning: to be, exist, have
Romaji: **a(ru)**
Phonetic: ah (roo)
Guide: 265

4b. 難しい
むずか

Meaning: to be difficult
Romaji: **muzuka(shii)**
Phonetic: moo zoo kah (shee ee)
Guide: 557

C. Misc. Actions その他の行動 Sono ta no ko-do-
た　こうどう

1. 稽古
けい こ

Meaning: practice; exercise; training
Romaji: **keiko**
Phonetic: kae ee koe
Guide: * 5d11.3, 172

1a. 稽
けい

Meaning: think, consider
Romaji: **kei**
Phonetic: kae ee
Guide: * 5d11.3

1b. 古い
ふる

Meaning: old
Romaji: **furui**
Phonetic: foo roo ee
Guide: 172

2. 氣合
き あい

Meaning: expelling breath and a shout from your lower abdomen as you execute a strike or technique to invoke your full spirit power
Romaji: **kiai**
Phonetic: kee ah ee
Guide: 134 (see page 8), 159 (see page 8)

3. 基本動作
<small>きほんどうさ</small>

Meaning: fundamental movement
Romaji: **kihondo-sa**
Phonetic: kee hoe n doe oo sah
Guide: 450, 25, 231, 360

3a. 基本
<small>き ほん</small>

Meaning: fundamental
Romaji: **kihon**
Phonetic: kee hoe n
Guide: 450, 25

3b. 基
<small>き</small>

Meaning: basis, foundation, origin
Romaji: **ki**
Phonetic: kee
Guide: 450

3c. 本
<small>ほん</small>

Meaning: origin; main
Romaji: **hon**
Phonetic: hoe n
Guide: 25

3d. 動作
<small>どうさ</small>

Meaning: movement
Romaji: **do-sa**
Phonetic: doe oo sah
Guide: 231, 360

3e. 動く
<small>うご</small>

Meaning: to move
Romaji: **ugo(ku)**
Phonetic: oo goe (koo)
Guide: 231

3f. 作る
<small>つく</small>

Meaning: to make
Romaji: **tsuku(ru)**
Phonetic: tsue koo (roo)
Guide: 360

4. 構え
_{かま}

Meaning: a posture
Romaji: **kama(e)**
Phonetic: kah mah (eh)
Guide: 1010

4a. 構える
_{かま}

Meaning: to take a posture in readiness
Romaji: **kama(eru)**
Phonetic: kah mah (eh roo)
Guide: 1010

5. 禊
_{みそぎ}

Meaning: purification
Romaji: **misogi**
Phonetic: mee soe gee
Guide: * 4e9.5

6. 黙想
_{もくそう}

Meaning: a form of meditation
Romaji: **mokuso-**
Phonetic: moe koo soe oo
Guide: 1578, 147

6a. 黙
_{もく}

Meaning: become silent, say nothing
Romaji: **moku**
Phonetic: moe koo
Guide: 1578

6b. 想
_{そう}

Meaning: idea, thought
Romaji: **so-**
Phonetic: soe oo
Guide: 147

It is recommended that all techniques be practiced equally on both the left and right sides. Likewise, many techniques are performed in two ways. First, going across uke's front and second, going to the rear of uke. Going across the front is "omote" and "ura" is to the rear.

おもて
7. 表

Meaning: the front
Romaji: **omote**
Phonetic: oe moe teh
Guide: 272

うら
8. 裏

Meaning: the rear
Romaji: **ura**
Phonetic: oo rah
Guide: 273

らん ど
9. 乱取り

Meaning: facing multiple attackers
Romaji: **rando(ri)**
Phonetic: rah n doe (ree)
Guide: 689, 65

らん
9a. 乱

Meaning: riot, rebellion; disorder
Romaji: **ran**
Phonetic: rah n
Guide: 689

と
9b. 取る

Meaning: to take
Romaji: **to(ru)**
Phonetic: toe (roo)
Guide: 65

れんしゅう
10. 練習

Meaning: practice
Romaji: **renshu-**
Phonetic: reh n shee yoo oo
Guide: 743, 591

れん
10a. 練

Meaning: train
Romaji: **ren**
Phonetic: reh n
Guide: 743

なら
10b. 習う

Meaning: to learn
Romaji: **nara(u)**
Phonetic: nah rah oo
Guide: 591

48

11. 四方切り
<small>し ほう ぎ</small>

Meaning: to cut in four directions – i.e.: N, S, E, W
Romaji: **shiho-gi(ri)**
Phonetic: shee hoe oo gee ree
Guide: 6, 70, 39

11a. 四方
<small>し ほう</small>

Meaning: four directions
Romaji: **shiho-**
Phonetic: shee hoe oo
Guide: 6, 70

11b. 切る
<small>き</small>

Meaning: to cut
Romaji: **ki(ru)**
Phonetic: kee roo
Guide: 39

12. 膝行
<small>しっこう</small>

Meaning: to walk on the knees
Romaji: **shikko-**
Phonetic: shee kkoe oo
Guide: * 4b11.4, 68

12a. 膝
<small>ひざ</small>

Meaning: knee
Romaji: **hiza**
Phonetic: hee zah
Guide: * 4b11.4

12b. 行う
<small>おこな</small>

Meaning: to go; do, perform, carry out
Romaji: **okona(u)**
Phonetic: oe koe nah oo
Guide: 68

13. 摺足
<small>すりあし</small>

Meaning: to move with lightly sliding one's feet
Romaji: **suriashi**
Phonetic: soo ree ah shee
Guide: * 3c11.3, 58

49

13a. 摺
<small>する</small>

Meaning: to rub
Romaji: **suru**
Phonetic: soo roo
Guide: * 3c11.3

13b. 足
<small>あし</small>

Meaning: feet
Romaji: **ashi**
Phonetic: ah shee
Guide: 58

14. 体裁き
<small>たいさば</small>

Meaning: body movements
Romaji: **taisaba(ki)**
Phonetic: tah ee sah bah kee
Guide: 61, 1123

14a. 体
<small>からだ</small>

Meaning: body
Romaji: **karada**
Phonetic: kah rah dah
Guide: 61

14b. 裁く
<small>さばく</small>

Meaning: pass judgement
Romaji: **saba(ku)**
Phonetic: sah bah koo
Guide: 1123

15. 転換
<small>てんかん</small>

Meaning: to turn
Romaji: **tenkan**
Phonetic: teh n kah n
Guide: 433, 1586

15a. 転ぶ
<small>ころ</small>

Meaning: to roll over
Romaji: **koro(bu)**
Phonetic: koe roe boo
Guide: 433

15b. 変える
<small>か</small>

Meaning: to substitute
Romaji: **ka(eru)**
Phonetic: kah eh roo
Guide: 1586

Chapter 8

Parts of the Body

<ruby>体<rt>からだ</rt></ruby> の <ruby>一部<rt>いちぶ</rt></ruby>

1. Ankle 足首 Ashikubi p. 52
2. Arm 腕 Ude p. 52
3. Back 背中 Senaka p. 52
4. Ear 耳 Mimi p. 52
5. Elbow 肘 Hiji p. 52
6. Eye 目 Me p. 52
7. Face 顔 Kao p. 52
8. Foot 足 Ashi p. 52
9. Hand 手 Te p. 52
10. Head 頭 Atama p. 52
11. Hips 腰 Koshi p. 52
12. Knee 膝 Hiza p. 53
13. Leg 足 Ashi p. 53
14. Mouth 口 Kuchi p. 53
15. Neck 首 Kubi p. 53
16. Nose 鼻 Hana p. 53
17. Shoulder 肩 Kata p. 53
18. Wrist 手首 Tekubi p. 53

あしくび
1. 足首
Meaning: ankle
Romaji: **ashikubi**
Phonetic: ah shee koo bee
Guide: 58, 148

あし
1a. 足
Meaning: leg/foot
Romaji: **ashi**
Phonetic: ah shee
Guide: 58

くび
1b. 首
Meaning: neck
Romaji: **kubi**
Phonetic: koo bee
Guide: 148

うで
2. 腕
Meaning: arm
Romaji: **ude**
Phonetic: oo dae
Guide: 1299

せなか
3. 背中
Meaning: back
Romaji: **senaka**
Phonetic: seh nah kah
Guide: 1265, 28

せ
3a. 背
Meaning: back
Romaji: **se**
Phonetic: seh
Guide: 1265

なか
3b. 中
Meaning: middle
Romaji: **naka**
Phonetic: nah kah
Guide: 28

みみ
4. 耳
Meaning: ear
Romaji: **mimi**
Phonetic: mee mee
Guide: 56

ひじ
5. 肘
Meaning: elbow
Romaji: **hiji**
Phonetic: hee jee
Guide: 4b3.3

め
6. 目
Meaning: eye
Romaji: **me**
Phonetic: mae
Guide: 55

かお
7. 顔
Meaning: face
Romaji: **kao**
Phonetic: kah oe
Guide: 277

あし
8.&13. 足
Meaning: foot, leg
Romaji: **ashi**
Phonetic: ah shee
Guide: 58

て
9. 手
Meaning: hand
Romaji: **te**
Phonetic: teh
Guide: 57

あたま
10. 頭
Meaning: head
Romaji: **atama**
Phonetic: ah tah mah
Guide: 276

こし
11. 腰
Meaning: hips, pelvic area
Romaji: **koshi**
Phonetic: koe shee
Guide: 1298

52

<ruby>12.<rt>ひざ</rt></ruby> 膝
Meaning: knee
Romaji: **hiza**
Phonetic: hee zah
Guide: * 4b11.4

13.&8. 足 (あし)
Meaning: foot, leg
Romaji: **ashi**
Phonetic: ah shee
Guide: 58

14. 口 (くち)
Meaning: mouth
Romaji: **kuchi**
Phonetic: koo chee
Guide: 54

15. 首 (くび)
Meaning: neck
Romaji: **kubi**
Phonetic: koo bee
Guide: 148

16. 鼻 (はな)
Meaning: nose
Romaji: **hana**
Phonetic: hah nah
Guide: 813

17. 肩 (かた)
Meaning: shoulder
Romaji: **kata**
Phonetic: kah tah
Guide: 1264

18. 手首 (てくび)
Meaning: wrist
Romaji: **tekubi**
Phonetic: teh koo bee
Guide: 57, 148

18a. 手 (て)
Meaning: hand
Romaji: **te**
Phonetic: teh
Guide: 57

18b. 首 (くび)
Meaning: neck
Romaji: **kubi**
Phonetic: koo bee
Guide: 148

This is the Okakoen (Oka Park) Aikido Dojo. The building is more than 100 years old. It has no air-conditioning and no heat – like most dojos in Japan. Awesome! Plus, O-sensei actually used this building for one of his early films. Cool. See page 90 for training times.

Chapter 9

Weapons - 武器(ぶき)

1. 30cm Knife 短刀(たんとう) tanto p. 56
2. Staff 杖(じょう) jo- p. 56
3. Sword 剣(けん) ken p. 56
4. Sword 刀(かたな) katana p. 56
5. Wooden Sword 木刀(ぼくとう) bokuto- p. 56

Aiki-Wear - 合氣道着(あいきどうぎ)の名称(めいしょう)

1. Belt 帯(おび) obi p. 56
2. Hakama 袴(はかま) hakama p. 56
3. Split-toed Socks 足袋(たび) tabi p. 57
4. Uniform 道着(どうぎ) do-gi p. 57

Ranks - 位(くらい)

1. Kyu 級(きゅう) kyu- p. 57
2. Dan 段(だん) dan p. 57
3. 1st – 10th Dan 初段(しょだん)から十段(じゅうだん)まで shodan kara ju-dan made p.58

Special Training – 特別訓練(とくべつくんれん)

1. Mid-Winter Training 寒稽古(かんげいこ) kangeiko p. 59
2. Mid-Summer Training 暑中稽古(しょちゅうけいこ) shochu-keiko p. 59

1. 短刀 たんとう

Meaning: a 30cm knife
Romaji: **tanto-**
Phonetic: tah n toe oo
Guide: 215, 37

1a. 短い みじか

Meaning: short
Romaji: **mijika(i)**
Phonetic: mee jee kah ee
Guide: 215

1b. 刀 とう

Meaning: sword, knife
Romaji: **to-**
Phonetic: toe oo
Guide: 37

2. 杖 じょう

Meaning: staff, cane
Romaji: **jo-**
Phonetic: joe oo
Guide: * 4a3.5

3. 剣 けん

Meaning: sword
Romaji: **ken**
Phonetic: ken
Guide: 879

4. 刀 かたな

Meaning: sword
Romaji: **katana**
Phonetic: kah tah nah
Guide: 37

5. 木刀 ぼくとう

Meaning: wooden sword
Romaji: **bokuto-**
Phonetic: boe koo toe oo
Guide: 22, 37

5a. 木 き

Meaning: tree, wood
Romaji: **ki**
Phonetic: kee
Guide: 22

Aiki-Wear - 合氣道着の名称 あいきどうぎ　めいしょう

1. 帯 おび

Meaning: belt
Romaji: **obi**
Phonetic: oe bee
Guide: 963

2. 袴 はかま

Meaning: formal pant-like portion of uniform
Romaji: **hakama**
Phonetic: ha kah mah
Guide: * 5e6.4

3. 足袋 <small>たび</small>
Meaning: Split-toed socks
Romaji: **tabi**
Phonetic: tah bee
Guide: 58, 1329

3a. 足 <small>あし</small>
Meaning: foot, leg
Romaji: **ashi**
Phonetic: ah shee
Guide: 58

3b. 袋 <small>ふくろ</small>
Meaning: bag, sack
Romaji: **fukuro**
Phonetic: foo koo roe
Guide: 1329

4. 道着 <small>どうぎ</small>
Meaning: uniform
Romaji: **Do-gi**
Phonetic: doe gee
Guide: 149, 657

4a. 道 <small>どう</small>
Meaning: street, way, path
Romaji: **do-**
Phonetic: doe
Guide: 149

4b. 着る <small>き</small>
Meaning: to wear
Romaji: **ki(ru)**
Phonetic: kee roo
Guide: 657

Ranks - 位 <small>くらい</small>

1. 級 <small>きゅう</small>
Meaning: rank, class
Romaji: **kyu-**
Phonetic: kee yoo
Guide: 568

2. 段 <small>だん</small>
Meaning: rank; step; stairs
Romaji: **dan**
Phonetic: dah n
Guide: 362

3. 初段から十段まで
<small>しょだん　　　　じゅうだん</small>

初段 shodan (1st degree black belt)

弐段 nidan (2nd degree black belt)

参段 sandan (3rd degree black belt)

四段 yodan (4th degree black belt)

五段 godan (5th degree black belt)

六段 rokudan (6th degree black belt)

七段 shichidan (7th degree black belt)

八段 hachidan (8th degree black belt)

九段 kudan (9th degree black belt)

十段 ju-dan (10th degree black belt)

Special Training – 特別訓練
<small>とくべつくんれん</small>

1. 寒稽古
<small>かんげいこ</small>

Meaning: Mid-winter training

Romaji: **kangeiko**

Phonetic: kah n geh ee koe

Guide: 457. * 5d11.3. 172

1a. 寒い
<small>さむ</small>

Meaning: cold

Romaji: **samui**

Phonetic: sah moo ee

Guide: 457

1b. 稽
<small>けい</small>

Meaning: think, consider; stop; reach; bow low

Romaji: **kei**

Phonetic: keh ee

Guide: * 5d11.3

1c. 古い
<small>ふる</small>

Meaning: old

Romaji: **furu(i)**

Phonetic: foo roo ee

Guide: 172

2. 暑中稽古
<small>しょちゅうけいこ</small>

Meaning: mid-summer training

Romaji: **shochu-keiko**

Phonetic: shoe choo kae ee koe

Guide: 638, 28, (* 5d11.3, 172 see above)

2a. 暑い
<small>あつ</small>

Meaning: hot (weather)

Romaji: **atsu(i)**

Phonetic: ah tsoo ee

Guide: 638

2b. 中
<small>ちゅう</small>

Meaning: middle

Romaji: **chu-**

Phonetic: choo

Guide: 28

This is the patch from my first dojo with Sensei David Monroe (www.sof-stx.com). As you can see – David combined the kanji used in martial arts which means, "The Way (to enlightenment)" along with the Christian cross –signifying that Jesus Christ is "The Way" to salvation.

Chapter 10

People – 人々(ひとびと)

1. Partner 相手 Aite p. 62
2. Understudy 弟子 Deshi p. 62
3. Live-in disciple 内弟子 Uchideshi p. 63
4. Head of Dojo 道場長 Do-jo-cho- p. 63
5. Head of Aikikai 道主 Do-shu p. 63
6. Junior student 後輩 Ko-hai p. 64
7. Senior student 先輩 Senpai p. 64
8. O-Sensei 翁先生 O-Sensei, Morihei Ueshiba – Founder of Aikido p. 64
9. Master of an art 師範 Shihan p. 65
10. One who performs the waza 取 Tori p. 65
11. One who receives during the performing of a waza 受 Uke p. 65
12. Practitioners having a "dan" ranking 有段者 Yu-dansha p. 66

61

1. 相手
あいて

Meaning: partner, opponent

Romaji: **aite**

Phonetic: ah ee teh

Guide: 146, 57

1a. 相
あい

Meaning: together, each other

Romaji: **ai**

Phonetic: ah ee

Guide: 146

1b. 手
て

Meaning: hand

Romaji: **te**

Phonetic: teh

Guide: 57

2. 弟子
でし

Meaning: understudy

Romaji: **deshi**

Phonetic: deh shee

Guide: 405, 103

2a. 弟
おとうと

Meaning: younger brother

Romaji: **oto-to**

Phonetic: oe toe oo toe

Guide: 405

2b. 子
し

Meaning: child

Romaji: **shi**

Phonetic: shee

Guide: 103

3. 内弟子
うちでし

Meaning: live-in understudy

Romaji: **uchi deshi**

Phonetic: oo chee deh shee

Guide: 84, 405, 103

3a. 内
うち

Meaning: inside

Romaji: **uchi**

Phonetic: oo chee

Guide: 84

4. 道 場 長
どうじょうちょう

Meaning: head of dojo

Romaji: **do-jo-cho-**

Phonetic: doe oo joe oo choe oo

Guide: 149, 154, 95

4a. 道
どう

Meaning: way, path

Romaji: **do-**

Phonetic: doe oo

Guide: 149

4b. 場
じょう

Meaning: place

Romaji: **jo-**

Phonetic: joe oo

Guide: 154

4c. 長
ちょう

Meaning: chief, head

Romaji: **cho-**

Phonetic: choe oo

Guide: 95

5. 道主
どうしゅ

Meaning: The head of Aikikai

Romaji: **do-shu**

Phonetic: doe oo shoo

Guide: 149, 155

5a. 道
どう

Meaning: street, way, path

Romaji: **do-**

Phonetic: doe oo

Guide: 149

5b. 主
しゅ

Meaning: main, principle

Romaji: **shu**

Phonetic: shoo

Guide: 155

こうはい
6. 後輩

Meaning: junior student

Romaji: **ko-hai**

Phonetic: koe oo hah ee

Guide: 48, 1037

うし
6a. 後ろ

Meaning: behind

Romaji: **ushi(ro)**

Phonetic: oo shee roe

Guide: 48

はい
6b. 輩

Meaning: colleague

Romaji: **hai**

Phonetic: hah ee

Guide: 1037

せんぱい
7. 先輩

Meaning: senior student

Romaji: **senpai**

Phonetic: she n pah ee

Guide: 50, 1037

おうせんせい
8. 翁先生

Meaning: the great teacher

Romaji: **o-sensei**

Phonetic: oe oo seh n seh ee

Guide: 1930, 50, 44

おう
8a. 翁

Meaning: old man

Romaji: **o-**

Phonetic: oe oo

Guide: 1930

せん
8b. 先

Meaning: earlier

Romaji: **sen**

Phonetic: seh n

Guide: 50

せい
8c. 生

Meaning: life

Romaji: **sei**

Phonetic: seh ee

Guide: 44

9. 師範
し はん

Meaning: master of an art

Romaji: **shihan**

Phonetic: shee hah n

Guide: 409, 1092

9a. 師
し

Meaning: teacher

Romaji: **shi**

Phonetic: shee

Guide: 409

9b. 範
はん

Meaning: example, model

Romaji: **han**

Phonetic: hah n

Guide: 1092

10. 取り
と

Meaning: performer of a waza

Romaji: **to(ri)**

Phonetic: toe ree

Guide: 65

10a. 取る
と

Meaning: to take

Romaji: **to(ru)**

Phonetic: toe roo

Guide: 65

11. 受
うけ

Meaning: receiver of a waza

Romaji: **uke**

Phonetic: oo keh

Guide: 260

11a. 受ける
う

Meaning: to receive

Romaji: **uke(ru)**

Phonetic: oo keh roo

Guide: 260

12. 有段者 <small>ゆうだんしゃ</small>

Meaning: those who possess a "dan" rank

Romaji: **yu-dansha**

Phonetic: yoo dah n shah

Guide: 265, 362, 164

12a. 有る <small>あ</small>

Meaning: be, exist, have

Romaji: **a(ru)**

Phonetic: ah roo

Guide: 265

12b. 段 <small>だん</small>

Meaning: level; rank

Romaji: **dan**

Phonetic: dah n

Guide: 362

12c. 者 <small>しゃ</small>

Meaning: person

Romaji: **sha**

Phonetic: shah

Guide: 164

Chapter 11

Places – 場所(ばしょ)

1. Workout hall 道場(どうじょう) Do-jo- p. 68
2. Headquarter dojo 本部道場(ほんぶどうじょう) Honbudo-jo- p. 68
3. Tanabe city 田辺市(たなべし) Tanabe shi p. 69
4. Wakayama prefecture 和歌山県(わかやまけん) Wakayama ken p. 70

1. 道場
<small>どうじょう</small>

Meaning: place of training

Romaji: **do-jo-**

Phonetic: doe oo joe oo

Guide: 149, 154

1a. 道
<small>どう</small>

Meaning: street, way, path

Romaji: **do-**

Phonetic: doe oo

Guide: 149

1b. 場
<small>じょう</small>

Meaning: place

Romaji: **jo-**

Phonetic: joe oo

Guide: 154

2. 本部道場
<small>ほんぶ どうじょう</small>

Meaning: headquarters

Romaji: **honbu do-jo-**

Phonetic: hoe n boo doe oo joe oo

Guide: 25, 86,149,154

2a. 本
<small>ほん</small>

Meaning: main

Romaji: **hon**

Phonetic: hoe n

Guide: 25

2b. 部
<small>ぶ</small>

Meaning: piece, part

Romaji: **bu**

Phonetic: boo

Guide: 86

3. 田辺市
<ruby>た</ruby><ruby>な</ruby><ruby>べ</ruby><ruby>し</ruby>

Meaning: Tanabe city - birthplace of O-sensei

Romaji: **Tanabe shi**

Phonetic: tah nah beh shee

Guide: 35, 445, 181

3a. 田
<ruby>た</ruby>

Meaning: rice field

Romaji: **ta**

Phonetic: tah

Guide: 35

3b. 辺
<ruby>なべ</ruby>

Meaning: near

Romaji: **nabe**

Phonetic: nah bae

Guide: 445

3c. 市
<ruby>し</ruby>

Meaning: city

Romaji: **shi**

Phonetic: shee

Guide: 181

4. 和歌山県
<small>わ か やま けん</small>

Meaning: Wakayama prefecture. Prefecture in which Tanabe city is located

Romaji: **Wakayama ken**

Phonetic: wah kah yah mah keh n

Guide: 124, 392, 34, 194

4a. 和
<small>わ</small>

Meaning: peace

Romaji: **wa**

Phonetic: wah

Guide: 124

4b. 歌
<small>か</small>

Meaning: song

Romaji: **ka**

Phonetic: kah

Guide: 392

4c. 山
<small>やま</small>

Meaning: mountain

Romaji: **yama**

Phonetic: yah mah

Guide: 34

4d. 県
<small>けん</small>

Meaning: prefecture

Romaji: **ken**

Phonetic: keh n

Guide: 194

Chapter 12
Miscellaneous

1. Aikido Organization 合氣会 Aikikai p. 73
2. Large Exhibition 演武大会 Enbutaikai p. 73
3. Combined exhibition 総合演武 So-do-enbu- p. 73,74
4. Lower level 下段 Gedan p. 74
5. Mid level 中段 Chu-dan p. 75
6. Upper level 上段 Jo-dan p. 75
7. Center 中心 Chu-shin p. 75
8. An axis (of rotation) 軸 Jiku p. 76
9. Center of gravity 重心 Ju-shin p. 76
10. Angle 角度 Kakudo p. 76
11. Triangle 三角 Sankaku p. 77
12. Square 四角 Shikaku p. 77
13. Round 丸い Marui p. 77
14. Proper distance 間合い Maai p. 78
15. Variation technique 変更技 Henko Waza p. 78
16. Paired fighting 組立 Kumitachi p. 79

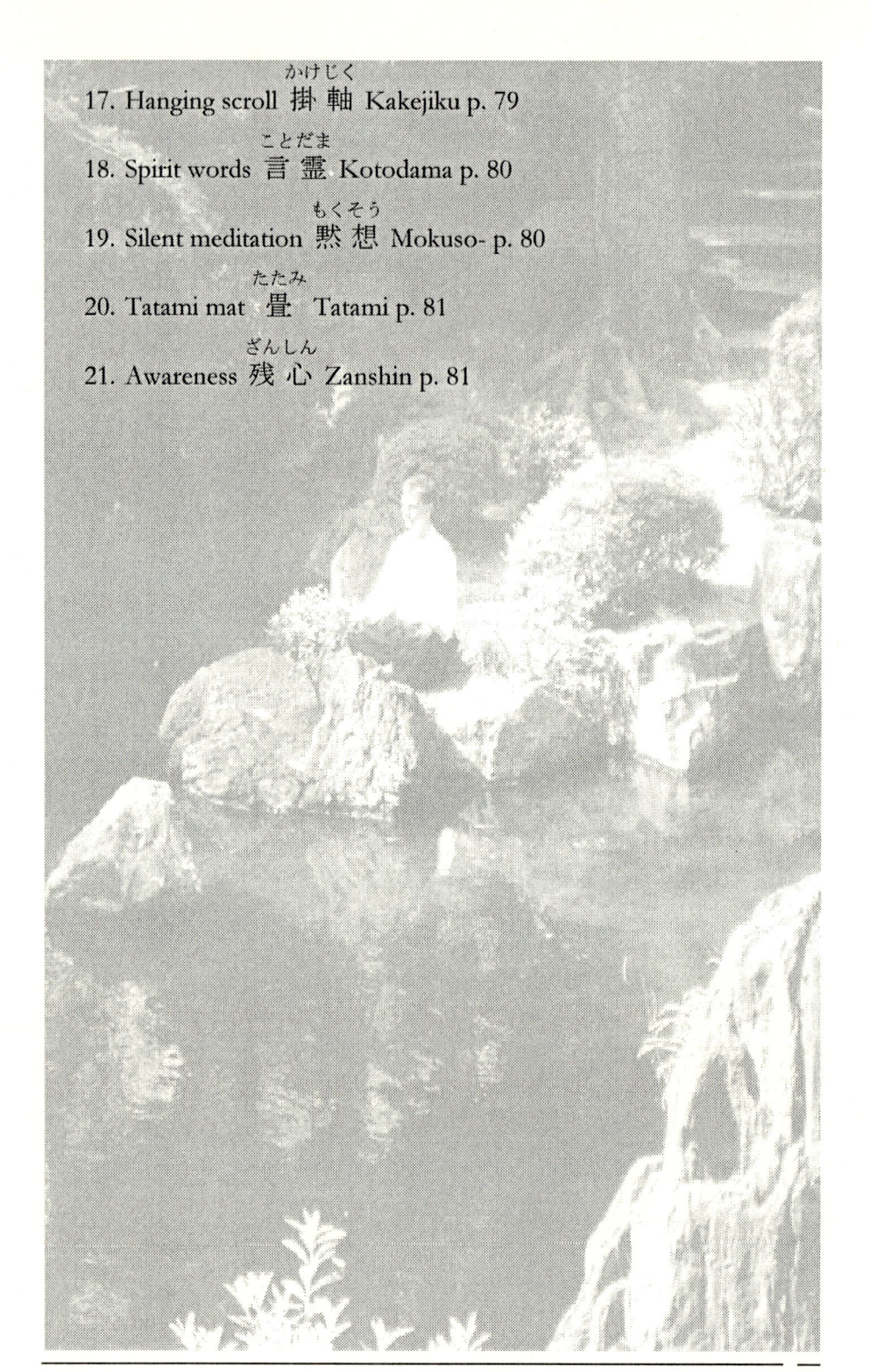

17. Hanging scroll 掛軸 Kakejiku p. 79
18. Spirit words 言霊 Kotodama p. 80
19. Silent meditation 黙想 Mokuso- p. 80
20. Tatami mat 畳 Tatami p. 81
21. Awareness 残心 Zanshin p. 81

あいきかい
1. 合氣会

Meaning: The Aikido organization
Romaji: **aikikai**
Phonetic: ah ee kee kah ee
Guide: 159, 134, 158

あ
1a. 合う

Meaning: to fit, put together
Romaji: **a(u)**
Phonetic: ah oo
Guide: 159

き
1b. 氣

Meaning: spirit, soul, mood
Romaji: **ki**
Phonetic: kee
Guide: 134

かい
1c. 会

Meaning: association
Romaji: **kai**
Phonetic: kah ee
Guide: 158

えんぶたいかい
2. 演武大会

Meaning: Large Exhibition
Romaji: **enbutaikai**
Phonetic: e n boo tah ee kah ee
Guide: 344, 1031, 26, 158 (see 1c. above)

えん
2a. 演

Meaning: performance
Romaji: **en**
Phonetic: eh n
Guide: 344

ぶ
2b. 武

Meaning: military
Romaji: **bu**
Phonetic: boo
Guide: 1031

たい
2c. 大

Meaning: large
Romaji: **tai**
Phonetic: tah ee
Guide: 26

そうごうえんぶ
3. 総合演武

Meaning: Combined Exhibition
Romaji: **so-go-enbu**
Phonetic: soe oo goe oo e n boo
Guide: 697, 159, 344, 1031 (see also 2a., 2b. above)

3a. 総
そう

Meaning: general
Romaji: **so-**
Phonetic: soe oo
Guide: 697

3b. 合
ごう

Meaning: put together
Romaji: **go-**
Phonetic: goe oo
Guide: 159

3c. 演
えん

Meaning: performance
Romaji: **en**
Phonetic: eh n
Guide: 344

3d. 武
ぶ

Meaning: military
Romaji: **bu**
Phonetic: boo
Guide: 1031

4. 下段
げだん

Meaning: lower level
Romaji: **gedan**
Phonetic: geh dah n
Guide: 31,362

4a. 下
げ

Meaning: lower part
Romaji: **ge**
Phonetic: geh
Guide: 31

4b. 段
だん

Meaning: step; stairs; rank
Romaji: **dan**
Phonetic: dah n
Guide: 362

5. 中段
<ruby>ちゅうだん</ruby>

Meaning: mid level
Romaji: **chu-dan**
Phonetic: choo dah n
Guide: 28,362

5a. 中
<ruby>ちゅう</ruby>

Meaning: middle
Romaji: **chu-**
Phonetic: choo
Guide: 28

5b. 段
<ruby>だん</ruby>

Meaning: step; stairs; rank
Romaji: **dan**
Phonetic: dah n
Guide: 362

6. 上段
<ruby>じょうだん</ruby>

Meaning: upper level
Romaji: **jo-dan**
Phonetic: joe dah n
Guide: 32,362

6a. 上
<ruby>じょう</ruby>

Meaning: upper part
Romaji: **jo-**
Phonetic: joe oo
Guide: 32

6b. 段
<ruby>だん</ruby>

Meaning: step; stairs; rank
Romaji: **dan**
Phonetic: dah n
Guide: 362

7. 中心
<ruby>ちゅうしん</ruby>

Meaning: center
Romaji: **chu-shin**
Phonetic: choo shee n
Guide: 28,97

7a. 中
<ruby>ちゅう</ruby>

Meaning: middle
Romaji: **chu-**
Phonetic: choo
Guide: 28

7b. 心
<ruby>こころ</ruby>

Meaning: heart, core
Romaji: **kokoro**
Phonetic: koe koe roe
Guide: 97

8. 軸
<small>じく</small>

Meaning: axis, shaft
Romaji: **jiku**
Phonetic: jee koo
Guide: 988
In Aikido — as to first create a center and then rotate around the resulting axis of rotation.

9. 重 心
<small>じゅうしん</small>

Meaning: center of gravity
Romaji: **ju-shin**
Phonetic: ji yoo shee n
Guide: 227, 97

9a. 重い
<small>おも</small>

Meaning: heavy
Romaji: **omo(i)**
Phonetic: oe moe ee
Guide: 227

9b. 心
<small>こころ</small>

Meaning: heart, core
Romaji: **kokoro**
Phonetic: koe koe roe
Guide: 97

10. 角度
<small>かくど</small>

Meaning: angle
Romaji: **kakudo**
Phonetic: kah koo doe
Guide: 473, 377

10a. 角
<small>かく</small>

Meaning: angle
Romaji: **kaku**
Phonetic: kah koo
Guide: 473

10b. 度
<small>ど</small>

Meaning: degree
Romaji: **do**
Phonetic: doe
Guide: 377

11. 三角 (さんかく)

Meaning: triangle
Romaji: **sankaku**
Phonetic: sah n kah koo
Guide: 4,473

11a. 三 (さん)

Meaning: three
Romaji: **san**
Phonetic: sah n
Guide: 4

11b. 角 (かく)

Meaning: angle
Romaji: **kaku**
Phonetic: kah koo
Guide: 473

12. 四角 (しかく)

Meaning: square
Romaji: **shikaku**
Phonetic: shee kah koo
Guide: 6,473

12a. 四 (し)

Meaning: four
Romaji: **shi**
Phonetic: shee
Guide: 6

12b. 角 (かく)

Meaning: angle
Romaji: **kaku**
Phonetic: kah koo
Guide: 473

13. 丸い (まるい)

Meaning: round
Romaji: **maru(i)**
Phonetic: mah roo ee
Guide: 644

14. 間合い
<ruby>ま</ruby> <ruby>あ</ruby>

Meaning: proper distance
Romaji: **maa(i)**
Phonetic: mah ah ee
Guide: 43,159

14a. 間
<ruby>ま</ruby>

Meaning: interval
Romaji: **ma**
Phonetic: mah
Guide: 43

14b. 合う
<ruby>あ</ruby>

Meaning: to put together
Romaji: **a(u)**
Phonetic: ah oo
Guide: 159

15. 変更技
<ruby>へんこうわざ</ruby>

Meaning: variation technique
Romaji: **henko-waza**
Phonetic: heh n koe oo wah zah
Guide: 257,1008,871

15a. 変える
<ruby>か</ruby>

Meaning: to change
Romaji: **ka(eru)**
Phonetic: kah eh roo
Guide: 257

15b. 更
<ruby>こう</ruby>

Meaning: anew
Romaji: **ko-**
Phonetic: koe oo
Guide: 1008

15c. 技
<ruby>わざ</ruby>

Meaning: technique
Romaji: **waza**
Phonetic: wah zah
Guide: 871

16. 組立ち
<small>くみた</small>

Meaning: paired fighting
Romaji: **kumita(chi)**
Phonetic: koo mee tah chee
Guide: 418, 121

16a. 組む
<small>く</small>

Meaning: to group
Romaji: **ku(mu)**
Phonetic: koo moo
Guide: 418

16b. 立つ
<small>た</small>

Meaning: to stand
Romaji: **ta(tsu)**
Phonetic: tah tsoo
Guide: 121

17. 掛け軸
<small>か じく</small>

Meaning: a hanging scroll
Romaji: **ka(ke)jiku**
Phonetic: kah keh jee koo
Guide: 1464, 988

17a. 掛ける
<small>か</small>

Meaning: to hang
Romaji: **ka(keru)**
Phonetic: kah keh roo
Guide: 1464

17b. 軸
<small>じく</small>

Meaning: axis, shaft
Romaji: **jiku**
Phonetic: jee koo
Guide: 988

18. 言霊 <small>ことだま</small>

Meaning: spirit words or words from the spirit
Romaji: **kotodama**
Phonetic: koe toe dah mah
Guide: 66,1168

18a. 言 <small>こと</small>

Meaning: word
Romaji: **koto**
Phonetic: koe toe
Guide: 66

18b. 霊 <small>たま</small>

Meaning: spirit, soul
Romaji: **tama**
Phonetic: tah mah
Guide: 1168

19. 黙想 <small>もくそう</small>

Meaning: silent meditation
Romaji: **mokuso-**
Phonetic: moe koo soe oo
Guide: 1578,147

19a. 黙 <small>もく</small>

Meaning: silent
Romaji: **moku**
Phonetic: moe koo
Guide: 1578

19b. 想 <small>そう</small>

Meaning: thought
Romaji: **so-**
Phonetic: soe oo
Guide: 147

20. 畳
<ruby>畳<rt>たたみ</rt></ruby>

Meaning: tatami mat
Romaji: **tatami**
Phonetic: tah tah mee
Guide: 1087

21. 残心
<ruby>残心<rt>ざんしん</rt></ruby>

Meaning: remaining aware of surroundings after completion of technique
Romaji: **zanshin**
Phonetic: zah n shee n
Guide: 650,97

21a. 残る
<ruby>残<rt>のこ</rt></ruby>

Meaning: to remain/leave behind
Romaji: **noko(ru)**
Phonetic: noe koe roo
Guide: 650

21b. 心
<ruby>心<rt>こころ</rt></ruby>

Meaning: heart; mind
Romaji: **kokoro**
Phonetic: koe koe roe
Guide: 97

INDEX by ROMAJI

Romaji	Japanese	English	Page	Guide
ai hanmi	相半身	same foot forward	15	146, 88, 59
aikido	合気道	art of Aikido	8	159, 134, 149
aikidoka	合気道家	practitioner	9	159, 134, 149, 165
aikikai	合気会	Aikido organization	73	159, 134,
aite	相手	partner	62	146, 57
arigato-gozaimasu	有難うございます	thank you	44,45	265, 557
ashi	足	foot/leg	52,53	58
ashikubi	足首	ankle	52	58, 148
atama	頭	head	52	276
atemi	当身	strikes	29	77, 59
bokuto-	木刀	wooden sword	56	22, 37
buki	武器	weapons	56	1031, 527
chu-dan	中段	mid level	75	28, 362
chu-shin	中心	center	75	28, 97
dan	段	level/rank	57	362
deshi	弟子	understudy	62	405, 103
do-gi	道着	aiki wear	57	149, 657
do-jo	道場	training hall	68	149, 154
do-jo-cho-	道場長	head of dojo	63	149, 154, 95
do-shu	道主	head of aikikai	63	149, 155
enbutaikai	演武大会	large exhibition	73	344, 1031, 26, 158
eri mochi	襟持ち	collar grab	23	1537, 451
furitama	振り玉	shaking down spirit	43	954, 1168
ganmen zuki	顔面突き	face punch	29	277, 274, 898
gedan	下段	lower level	74	31, 362
godan	五段	5th degree	58	7, 362
gyaku hanmi	逆半身	opposite stance	16	444, 88, 59
hachidan	八段	8th degree	58	10, 362
hakama	袴	aiki pants	56	* 5e6.4
hana	鼻	nose	53	813
hanmi	半身	half-facing stance	12	88, 59
hanmi han dachi waza	半身半立ち技	one standing/sitting	35	88, 59, 88, 121, 871
henko- waza	変更技	variation technique	78	257, 1008, 871
hidari hanmi	左半身	left-facing stance	14	75, 88, 59
hiji	肘	elbow	52	* 4b3.3
hiza	膝	knee	53	* 4b11.4
honbudojo	本部道場	main aikido dojo	68	25, 86, 149, 154

82

ikkyo- osae	一教押さえ	first control	35,36	2, 245, 986
irimi nage	入り身投げ	entering throw	38	52, 59, 1021
jiku	軸	axle	76	988
jo-	杖	staff	56	*4a3.5
jo-dan	上段	upper level	75	32, 362
ju-dan	十段	10th degree	58	12, 362
ju-shin	重心	center of gravity	76	227, 97
kakejiku	掛け軸	hanging scroll	79	1464, 988
kakeru	掛	hang up	79	1464
kakudo	角度	angle	76	473, 377
kamae	構え	stance	47	1010
kangeiko	寒稽古	mid-winter training	59	457, * 5d11.3, 172
kao	顔	face	52	277
kata	肩	shoulder	53	1264
katame waza	固め技	fixed technique	34	972, 871
katana	刀	sword	56	37
katate mochi	片手持ち	one-handed grasp	19	1045, 57, 451
keiko	稽古	practice	45	* 5d11.3, 172
ken	剣	sword	56	879
keri	蹴り	kick	29	* 7d12.2
kiai	気合	shout	45	134, 159
kihondo-sa	基本動作	fundamental technique	46	450, 25, 231, 360
kogi bune undo	漕ぎ舟運動	rowing the boat	42	* 3a11.7, 376,439,231
ko-hai	後輩	junior student	64	48, 1037
kokyu- nage	呼吸投げ	breathe throw	39	1254, 1256, 1021
ko-sa mochi	交差持ち	cross-hand grasp	21	114, 658, 451
koshi	腰	waist	52	1298
koshi nage	腰投げ	waist/hip throw	39	1298, 1021
kotegaeshi	小手返し	writst throw	37	27, 274, 442
kotodama	言霊	spirit words	80	66, 1168
kubi	首	neck	53	148
kuchi	口	mouth	53	54
kudan	九段	9th degree	58	11, 362
kumitachi	組立ち	paired fighting	79	418, 121
kyu-	級	rank	57	568
maai	間合い	proper distance	78	43, 159
mae ukemi	前受身	forward roll	32	47, 260, 59
marui	丸い	round	77	644
me	目	eye	52	55
migi hanmi	右半身	right-facing stance	13	76, 88, 59
mimi	耳	ear	52	56

misogi	禊	purification by water	47	*4e9.5
mochi kata	持ち方	grasping method	18	451, 70
mokuso-	黙想	silent meditation	47,80	1578, 147
morote mochi	諸手持ち	two-handed grasp	22	861, 57, 451
nagare waza	流れ技	flowing techniques	34	247, 871
nidan	二段	2nd degree	58	3, 362
nikyo- osae	二教押さえ	second control	35,36	3, 245, 986
obi	帯	belt	56	963
omote	表	front	48	272
onegaishimasu	お願いします	please	44	581
o-sensei	翁先生	Morihei Ueshiba	64	1930, 50, 44
randori	乱取り	round robin	48	689, 65
rei	礼	bow	44	620
renshu-	練習	practice	48	743, 591
rokudan	六段	6th degree	58	8, 362
ryote mochi	両手持ち	two-handed grasp	20	200, 57, 451
sandan	三段	3rd degree	58	4, 362
sankaku	三角	triangle	77	4, 473
sankyo- osae	三教押さえ	third control	35,36	4, 245, 986
seiza	正座	sitting	44	275, 786
senaka	背中	back	52	1265, 28
senpai	先輩	senior student	64	50, 1037
shichidan	七段	7th degree	58	9, 362
shihan	師範	master	65	409, 1092
shiho-giri	四方切り	four direction cut	49	6, 70, 39
shiho-nage	四方投げ	four direction throw	37	6, 70, 1021
shikaku	四角	square	77	6, 473
shikko-	膝行	knee walking	49	*4b11.4, 68
shochu-keiko	暑中稽古	mid-summer training	59	638, 28, *5d11.3, 172
shodan	初段	1st degree	58	679, 362
sho-men uchi	正面打ち	frontal strike	27	275, 274, 1020
so-go-enbu-	総合演武	combined exhibition	73,74	697, 159, 344, 1031
suriashi	摺足	sliding feet	49,50	*3c11.3, 58
suwari waza	座り技	sitting technique	34	786, 871
tabi	足袋	split-toed socks	57	58, 1329
tachi waza	立ち技	standing technique	34	121, 871
taisabaki	体裁き	body movements	50	61, 1123
tanabe-shi	田辺市	Tanabe city	69	35, 445, 181
tanto-	短刀	short sword	56	215, 37
tatami	畳	tatami mat	81	1087
te	手	hand	52	57

84

tekubi	手首	wrist	53	57, 148
tenchi nage	天地投げ	heaven/earth throw	38	141, 118, 1021
tenkan	転換	turning	50	433, 1586
tori	取り	performer	65	65
tsuki	突き	punch	29	898
uchi kata	打ち方	striking method	26	1020, 70
uchideshi	内弟子	live-in disciple	63	84, 405, 103
ude	腕	arm	52	1299
uke	受け	receiver	65	260
ukemi	受身	falls	32	260, 59
ura	裏	rear	48	273
ushiro dori	後取り	grasp from beind	24	48, 65
ushiro ukemi	後受身	backward roll	32	260, 59
wakayama-ken	和歌県	Wakayama prefecture	70	124, 392, 34, 181
yodan	四段	4th degree	58	6, 362
yokomen uchi	横面打ち	diagonal strike	28	781, 274, 1020
yonkyo- osae	四教押さえ	fourth control	35,36	6, 245, 986
yu-dansha	有段者	possessor of black belt	66	265, 362, 164
zanshin	残心	awareness	81	650, 97

* *Japanese Character Dictionary – With Compound Lookup via Any Kanji* by Mark Spahn & Wolfgang Hadamitzky, Nichigai Associates 1989, ISBN 4-8169-0828-5

INDEX by ENGLISH

English	Japanese	Romaji	Page	Guide
1st degree	初段	shodan	58	679, 362
2nd degree	二段	nidan	58	3, 362
3rd degree	三段	sandan	58	4, 362
4th degree	四段	yodan	58	6, 362
5th degree	五段	godan	58	7, 362
6th degree	六段	rokudan	58	8, 362
7th degree	七段	shichidan	58	9, 362
8th degree	八段	hachidan	58	10, 362
9th degree	九段	kudan	58	11, 362
10th degree	十段	ju-dan	58	12, 362
aiki pants	袴	hakama	56	* 5e6.4
aiki wear	道着	do-gi	57	149, 657
Aikido organization	合気会	aikikai	73	159, 134,
angle	角度	kakudo	76	473, 377
ankle	足首	ashikubi	52	58, 148
arm	腕	ude	52	1299
art of Aikido	合気道	aikido	8	159, 134, 149
awareness	残心	zanshin	81	650, 97
axle	軸	jiku	76	988
back	背中	senaka	52	1265, 28
backward roll	後受身	ushiro ukemi	32	260, 59
belt	帯	obi	56	963
body movements	体裁き	taisabaki	50	61, 1123
bow	礼	rei	44	620
breathe throw	呼吸投げ	kokyu- nage	39	1254, 1256, 1021
center	中心	chu-shin	75	28, 97
center of gravity	重心	ju-shin	76	227, 97
collar grab	襟持ち	eri mochi	23	1537, 451
combined exhibition	総合演武	so-go-enbu-	73,74	697, 159, 344, 1031
cross-hand grasp	交差持ち	ko-sa mochi	21	114, 658, 451
diagonal strike	横面打ち	yokomen uchi	28	781, 274, 1020
ear	耳	mimi	52	56
elbow	肘	hiji	52	* 4b3.3
entering throw	入り身投げ	irimi nage	38	52, 59, 1021
eye	目	me	52	55
face	顔	kao	52	277
face punch	顔面突き	ganmen zuki	29	277, 274, 898

86

English	Kanji	Romaji	Page	References
falls	受身	ukemi	32	260, 59
first control	一教押さえ	ikkyo-osae	35,36	2, 245, 986
fixed technique	固め技	katame waza	34	972, 871
flowing techniques	流れ技	nagare waza	34	247, 871
foot/leg	足	ashi	52,53	58
forward roll	前受身	mae ukemi	32	47, 260, 59
four direction cut	四方切り	shiho-giri	49	6, 70, 39
four direction throw	四方投げ	shiho-nage	37	6, 70, 1021
fourth control	四教押さえ	yonkkyo-osae	35,36	6, 245, 986
front	表	omote	48	272
frontal strike	正面打ち	sho-men uchi	27	275, 274, 1020
fundamental technique	基本動作	kihondo-sa	46	450, 25, 231, 360
grasp from beind	後取り	ushiro dori	24	48, 65
grasping method	持ち方	mochi kata	18	451, 70
half-facing stance	半身	hanmi	12	88, 59
hand	手	te	52	57
hang up	掛	kakeru	79	1464
hanging scroll	掛け軸	kakejiku	79	1464, 988
head	頭	atama	52	276
head of aikikai	道主	do-shu	63	149, 155
head of dojo	道場長	do-jo-cho-	63	149, 154, 95
heaven/earth throw	天地投げ	tenchi nage	38	141, 118, 1021
junior student	後輩	ko-hai	64	48, 1037
kick	蹴り	keri	29	*7d12.2
knee	膝	hiza	53	*4b11.4
knee walking	膝行	shikko-	49	*4b11.4, 68
large exhibition	演武大会	enbutaikai	73	344, 1031, 26, 158
left-facing stance	左半身	hidari hanmi	14	75, 88, 59
level/rank	段	dan	57	362
live-in disciple	内弟子	uchideshi	63	84, 405, 103
lower level	下段	gedan	74	31, 362
main aikido dojo	本部道場	honbudojo	68	25, 86, 149, 154
master	師範	shihan	65	409, 1092
mid level	中段	chu-dan	75	28, 362
mid-summer training	暑中稽古	shochu-keiko	59	638, 28, *5d11.3, 172
mid-winter training	寒稽古	kangeiko	59	457, *5d11.3, 172
Morihei Ueshiba	翁先生	o-sensei	64	1930, 50, 44
mouth	口	kuchi	53	54
neck	首	kubi	53	148
nose	鼻	hana	53	813
one standing/sitting	半身半立ち技	hanmi han dachi waza	35	88, 59, 88, 121, 871

87

English	Kanji	Romaji	Page	References
one-handed grasp	片手持ち	katate mochi	19	1045, 57, 451
opposite stance	逆半身	gyaku hanmi	16	444, 88, 59
paired fighting	組立ち	kumitachi	79	418, 121
partner	相手	aite	62	146, 57
performer	取り	tori	65	65
please	お願いします	onegaishimasu	44	581
possessor of black belt	有段者	yu-dansha	66	265, 362, 164
practice	稽古	keiko	45	* 5d11.3, 172
practice	練習	renshu-	48	743, 591
practitioner	合気道家	aikidoka	9	159, 134, 149, 165
proper distance	間合い	maai	78	43, 159
punch	突き	tsuki	29	898
purification by water	禊	misogi	47	* 4e9.5
rank	級	kyu-	57	568
rear	裏	ura	48	273
receiver	受け	uke	65	260
right-facing stance	右半身	migi hanmi	13	76, 88, 59
round	丸い	marui	77	644
round robin	乱取り	randori	48	689, 65
rowing the boat	漕ぎ舟運動	kogi bune undo	42	* 3a11.7, 376,439,231
same foot forward	相半身	ai hanmi	15	146, 88, 59
second control	二教押さえ	nikyo- osae	35,36	3, 245, 986
senior student	先輩	senpai	64	50, 1037
shaking down spirit	振り玉	furitama	43	954, 1168
short sword	短刀	tanto-	56	215, 37
shoulder	肩	kata	53	1264
shout	気合	kiai	45	134, 159
silent meditation	黙想	mokuso-	47,80	1578, 147
sitting	正座	seiza	44	275, 786
sitting technique	座り技	suwari waza	34	786, 871
sliding feet	摺足	suriashi	49,50	* 3c11.3, 58
spirit words	言霊	kotodama	80	66, 1168
split-toed socks	足袋	tabi	57	58, 1329
square	四角	shikaku	77	6, 473
staff	杖	jo-	56	* 4a3.5
stance	構え	kamae	47	1010
standing technique	立ち技	tachi waza	34	121, 871
strikes	当身	atemi	29	77, 59
striking method	打ち方	uchi kata	26	1020, 70
sword	刀	katana	56	37
sword	剣	ken	56	879

88

English	Kanji	Romaji	Page	References
Tanabe city	田辺市	tanabe-shi	69	35, 445, 181
tatami mat	畳	tatami	81	1087
thank you	有難うございます	arigato-gozaimasu	44, 45	265, 557
third control	三教押さえ	sankyo- osae	35, 36	4, 245, 986
training hall	道場	do-jo	68	149, 154
triangle	三角	sankaku	77	4, 473
turning	転換	tenkan	50	433, 1586
two-handed grasp	諸手持ち	morote mochi	22	861, 57, 451
two-handed grasp	両手持ち	ryote mochi	20	200, 57, 451
understudy	弟子	deshi	62	405, 103
upper level	上段	jo-dan	75	32, 362
variation technique	変更技	henko- waza	78	257, 1008, 871
waist	腰	koshi	52	1298
waist/hip throw	腰投げ	koshi nage	39	1298, 1021
Wakayama prefecture	和歌県	wakayama-ken	70	124, 392, 34, 181
weapons	武器	buki	56	1031, 527
wooden sword	木刀	bokuto-	56	22, 37
wrist	手首	tekubi	53	57, 148
writst throw	小手返し	kotegaeshi	37	27, 274, 442

* *Japanese Character Dictionary – With Compound Lookup via Any Kanji* by Mark Spahn & Wolfgang Hadamitzky, Nichigai Associates 1989, ISBN 4-8169-0828-5

Credits

Kanji & Kana, A Handbook of the Japanese Writing System by Wolfgang Hadamitzky & Mark Spahn, Tuttle Publishing 2002, ISBN 0-8048-2077-5 www.tuttlepublishing.com

Japanese Character Dictionary – With Compound Lookup via Any Kanji by Mark Spahn & Wolfgang Hadamitzky, Nichigai Associates 1989, ISBN 4-8169-0828-5

Okakoen, Koshito Ichiichi Aikido Dojo, Wakayama city, Japan.

Practice:

- Monday, Tuesday, Thursday, Friday, Saturday 6-7pm.
- Monday, Wednesday, Friday 6:30-7:30am.
- Sunday 8:30-9:30am.

Eight Winds Aikido Society, 2404 Ladnier Road, Gautier, Mississippi 39553. Phone 228-497-9899. Shihan Carmen Pelusi.

Practice:

- Tuesday, Friday 7-9pm.

Photography: Miyako Taylor

Model: Katsumi Sakai, Aru Animal Hospital, Wakayama city, Japan www.aruah.com

Join the author's Aikido club online!
http://sports.groups.yahoo.com/group/aikido2/

Email the author: kinbo2004@earthlink.net

And finally…It's all about the icecream!

But always be prepared for an attack!

Out of respect for and thanks to all of my friends at the Eight Winds Aikido Society...

Printed in the United Kingdom
by Lightning Source UK Ltd.
108100UKS00001B/157